The Deep Green Planet

THE TROPICAL FOREST

The Deep Green Planet

THE TROPICAL FOREST

Renato Massa

English translation by Neil Frazer Davenport

RSVP
**RAINTREE
STECK-VAUGHN**
PUBLISHERS
The Steck-Vaughn Company

Austin, Texas

Published by Raintree Steck-Vaughn Publishers, an imprint of Steck-Vaughn Company

Editors
Caterina Longanesi, Linda Zierdt-Warshaw

Design and layout
Jaca Book Design Office

Library of Congress Cataloging-in-Publication Data

Massa, Renato.
    [Foresta tropicale. English]
    The tropical forest / Renato Massa.
       p.   cm. — (The Deep green planet)
    Includes bibliographical references (p.57) and index.
    Summary: Discusses the environment of a tropical forest and the different types of vegetation and animal life that thrive there.
    ISBN 0-8172-4311-9
    1. Rain forest ecology — Juvenile literature.   2. Rain forest animals — Juvenile literature.
3. Rain forest plants — Juvenile literature.   4. Rain forest — Juvenile literature.   [1. Rain forests.   2. Rain forest animals.   3. Rain forest plants.   4. Rain forest ecology.   5. Ecology.]
I. Title.   II. Series.
QH541.5.R27M3813   1997
574.5'2642 — dc20

96–28547
CIP   AC

Printed and bound in the United States
1 2 3 4 5 6 7 8 9 0 WO 99 98 97 96

CONTENTS

INTRODUCTION

On October 9, 1987, a NASA satellite orbiting Earth photographed the Amazon basin from space. The picture transmitted to the ground showed a half-moon shape of dense white dots on a black background. To those not accustomed to the techniques and interpretation of satellite photography, the picture may have been mistaken for a magnificent view of the galaxy. However, each of the white dots was not a star. Rather, it was a fire in the tropical forest. About 2,500 forest fires burned at the same time in the ravaged state of Rondonia in Brazil. A total of 7,603 burned throughout the great river basin. Scientists received live images of the greatest tragedy currently afflicting our planet—the accelerating destruction of the tropical forests. Over the past century, people have been wiping out one of the oldest and richest ecosystems the world has ever seen. In the process, an immense variety of plant and animal species, half of all the species that live on the Earth today, are being destroyed. People are changing the immense biomass into a lethal cloud of smoke and carbon dioxide.

The tropical forests are the original lost paradise, a great reserve of renewable biological resources, a system for ensuring a stable planetary climate, and an evolutionary vessel.

One of the greatest challenges facing humanity over the next hundred years is that of restoring, as far as possible, the forests and all that they represent for human society. To achieve this goal, humanity will have to convince itself that this is what it really wants. In the meantime, it will be up to a group of scientists, the conservation biologists, to attempt to preserve as much of the basic material needed for the task as possible. This material ranges from fragmented areas of forest floating in a sea of agricultural and urban development, to minute animal populations in constant danger of complete collapse. There are plants that for millions of years have adapted to the shady depths of the jungle and are now threatened on all sides by the encroachment of open areas. This ecological heritage will have to be guarded like a sacred flame in the hearth of a prehistoric cavern if it is to be maintained and eventually restored to its former glory.

The forests will return one day. They will have to return if we want to guarantee a future for our planet. In the geological history of the Earth, there have been eras in which the forests regressed. The era in which we are living should also be no more than an episode, a terrible episode, to be relegated among the nightmares of the past as soon as possible.

RENATO MASSA

THE TROPICAL FORESTS

A Prehistoric Community
Tropical rain forests are among Earth's oldest forest communities. These diverse forests date back at least 65 million years, to a time when dinosaurs still roamed the planet. They are called tropical rain forests because they are located in the wettest regions of the Earth, between the Tropic of Cancer and the Tropic of Capricorn on either side of the equator.

Tropical rain forests exist in Africa, Madagascar, Southeast Asia, Indonesia, New Guinea, and Oceania. They are also located in Central and South America. Together, tropical rain forests once covered about 20 percent of Earth's dry land. They continued to do so until the early twentieth century. Today, the rain forests cover only about 6 percent of the Earth's dry land. Regardless, they continue to support about 50 percent of Earth's animal and plant species.

Plentiful, Well-Distributed Rainfall
The amazing number of species in tropical rain forests results from many favorable factors. In areas of tropical rainfall, the average annual temperature is 26 to 27°C (79 to 81°F). There is never less than 1,500 millimeters (59 inches) of rain each year. The total rainfall is often greater than 2,000 millimeters (80 inches) and may even be 4,000 to 7,000 millimeters (157 to 276 inches) in some areas.

In the true rain forest, rainfall is abundant and fairly evenly distributed throughout the year. The dry season never lasts more than a few months. Beyond this limit, the

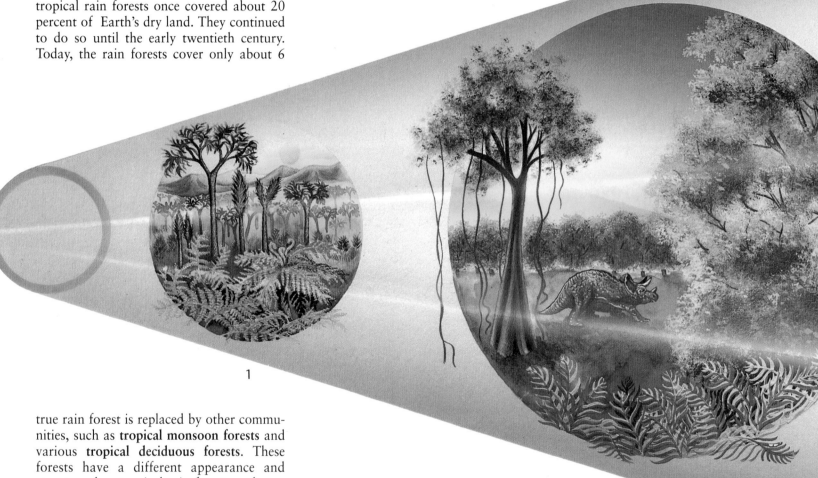

1

2

true rain forest is replaced by other communities, such as **tropical monsoon forests** and various **tropical deciduous forests**. These forests have a different appearance and structure than tropical rain forests and contain species of trees that lose their leaves during the dry season.

In mountainous tropical areas, the rain forest changes as you climb higher. The true rain forest is replaced by various types of **tropical mountain forests**. These forests have a large range of typical species that often grow in only one definite region.

A Rapid, Fragile Cycle
The hot, wet climate of tropical rain forests normally guarantees that these forests are very fertile. The temperature and humidity of

A history of our planet's tropical forests.
1. The forest of the Carboniferous period, 280 to 345 million years ago, was composed of plant species very different from those we know today.
2. In the late Cretaceous period, about 70 million years ago, we find seed plants and a landscape that hardly seems prehistoric except for the presence of dinosaurs, here represented by a *Triceratops*. **3.** In the last circle, a modern tropical forest, Otway Ranges of northern Australia.

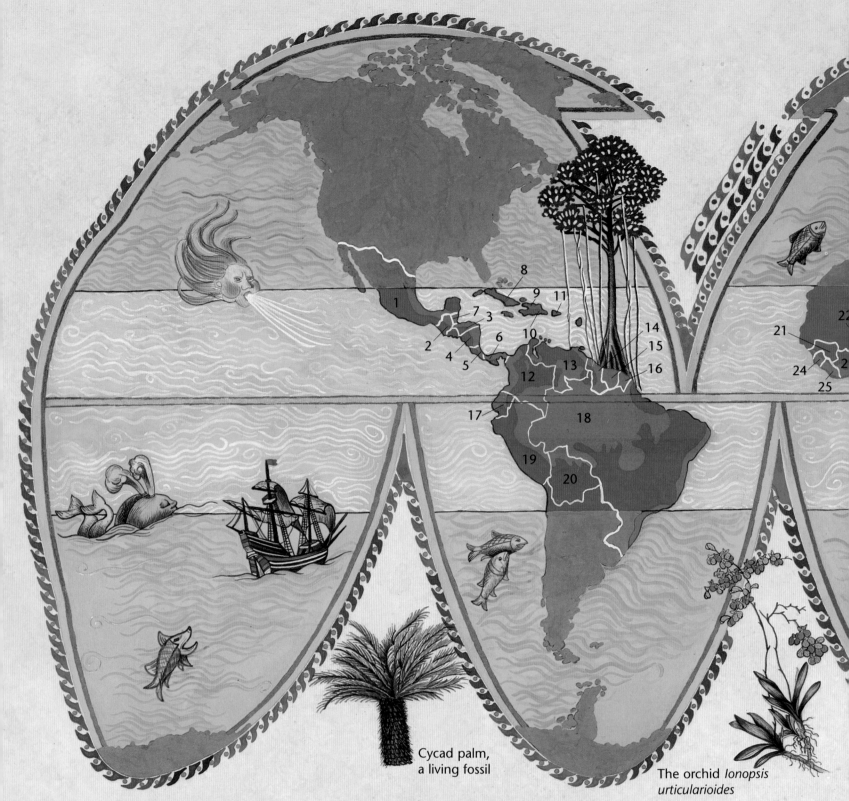

Cycad palm,
a living fossil

The orchid *Ionopsis
urticularioides*

The location of the world's tropical rain forests.

CENTRAL AND NORTH AMERICA **1**. Mexico: the last tropical forests, on the borders with Guatemala, are rapidly being destroyed by farmers. **2**. Guatemala **3**. Honduras **4**. Nicaragua **5**. Costa Rica **6**. Panama **7**. Belize: progressive expansion of livestock farming and a loss of forest areas; some small areas are protected as parks. THE CARIBBEAN **8**. Cuba **9**. Haiti **10**. Dominican Republic **11**. Puerto Rico: forests reduced to minimal areas due to the high population density.

SOUTH AMERICA **12**. Colombia: one-third of the country is covered by forests. **13**. Venezuela: vast areas still intact in the south, livestock and farmland expanding in the north. **14**. Guyana: population concentrated along the coasts. The forests are almost intact. **15**. Surinam: much of the forest protected in parks and reserves. **16**. French Guiana: population concentrated along the coasts. The forests are almost intact. **17**. Ecuador: much of the forest along the Pacific Ocean has been destroyed. **18**. Brazil: forests almost completely destroyed in the northeast, clearly

reduced in the south. **19**. Peru: vast areas of forest destroyed by livestock farming. **20**. Bolivia: areas of forest intact, now threatened by roads, farms, and livestock. AFRICA **21**. Guinea: fragments in the southwest. **22**. Ghana: forests almost completely destroyed by farmers; fragments in the southwest. **23**. Benin: three-quarters of the forests intact but threatened by rapid population growth. **24**. Sierra Leone: forests largely destroyed by nomadic agriculture. **25**. Liberia: forests almost destroyed by nomadic agriculture. **26**. Ivory Coast: more than 70 percent

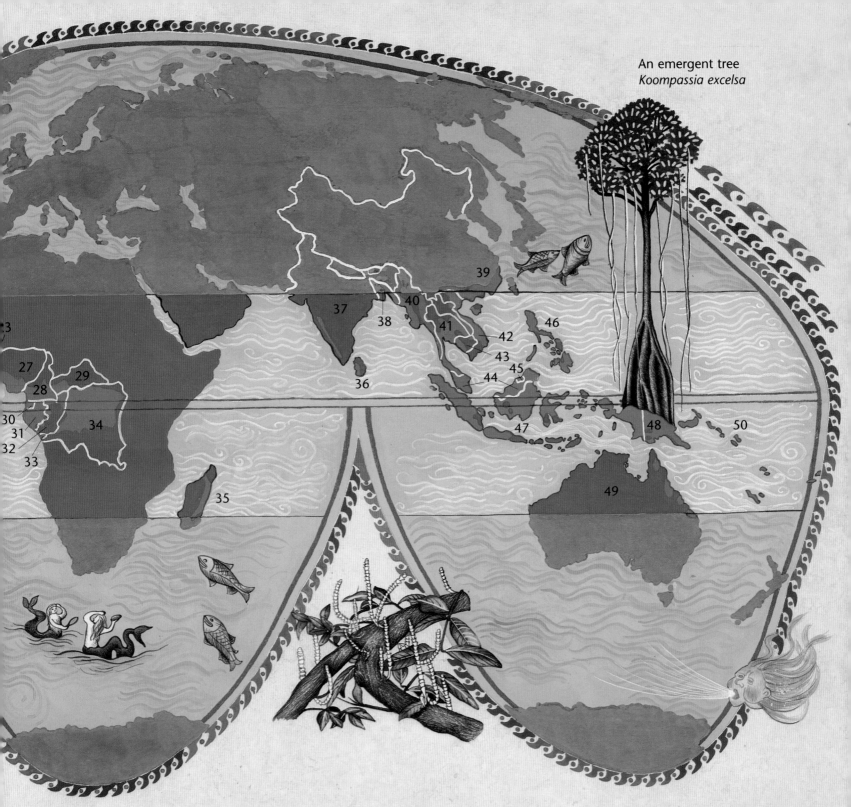

An emergent tree
Koompassia excelsa

of the forest existing at the turn of the 20th century destroyed by the logging industry and agriculture. **27**. Nigeria: forest almost entirely destroyed by the logging industry. **28**. Cameroon: destruction of forests, especially in southwest by nomadic agriculture and logging. **29**. Central African Republic: forest almost completely intact in the south. **30**. Equatorial Guinea: well covered with forests having good conservation prospects. **31**. Gabon: almost entirely covered with forests, destruction just beginning. **32**. Congo: logging industry in the south; forests undisturbed in the

more remote northern and central regions. **33**. Angola: fragments in the north. **34**. Zaire: the largest area of African tropical forest, a tenth of the world's total. Destruction generally limited to nomadic agriculture. **35**. Madagascar: forests largely destroyed by farmers. Asia **36**. Sri Lanka **37**. India: protected areas in Malabar **38**. Bangladesh **39**. China: much of the tropical forest destroyed. Small protected areas in southern China. **40**. Burma **41**. Thailand **42**. Vietnam **43**. Cambodia: only small areas of forest remain. **44**. Malaysia:

two-thirds of the original forest converted into agricultural land. **45**. Brunei: vast areas intact. **46**. The Philippines: forests reduced by two-thirds over the last 30 years. **47**. Indonesia: vast areas of forest, about one-tenth of the world's total, but wide-scale destruction in progress. **48**. Papua New Guinea: vast areas intact. Australia **49**. Fragments along the eastern coasts of Queensland. **50**. Solomon Islands: three-quarters covered by forests, generally in steeply sloping areas.

rain forests cause dead plants and animals to decompose rapidly. Thus, a constant supply of essential plant **nutrients**, such as **nitrogen**, **phosphorous**, and **potassium**, is abundant. Rain forest plants find the nutrients they need in the first 100 to 120 centimeters (39 to 47 inches) of soil, eliminating the need for their roots to penetrate far into the ground. Plants having deep roots do not gain an advantage because below the first **fertile layer** lies a practically **sterile layer** that is about 10 meters (33 feet) deep. This sterile layer is made up of **eroded** rock that is rich in **iron oxides**. Rain forest plants rapidly take in all the nutrients they find in the **topsoil**, which is populated by countless **fungi decomposers**. The plants change the material into living tissue so quickly that few nutrients are washed away by the rain.

The rapid growth of rain forest plants keeps a large number of buds, leaves, flowers, fruits, and other plant material constantly available. These nutrient reserves are used by many different animals. These animals differ from one continent to the next and from one forest to the next in the same continent or even the same region.

The growth cycle of tropical rain forest plants is rapid and efficient. It is also very fragile. If the forest is destroyed, the source of new organic matter for the 120 centimeters (47 inches) of fertile soil is eliminated. The remaining **organic matter** rapidly decomposes and is soon exhausted. **Inorganic** nutrients formed through decomposition barely support a few brief agricultural growing seasons. The remaining soil becomes dry and sterile. This soil is the same as the sterile soil found below the organic layer that once supported the lush vegetation that provided countless animals with food, shelter, and all the resources that they needed to live.

Below: An aerial view of the meandering Marañon River in Peru. In spite of the relatively poor soils, if the tropical rain forest is left undisturbed, it grows vigorously and is complex.

Right: A comparison of the soils of a temperate forest and those of a tropical forest, illustrating the consequences of using the land for agriculture. In the temperate forest, the humus layer is deep enough to last for some time after deforestation, unless it is washed away. In the tropical forest, the humus layer is only 100 to 120 centimeters (39 to 47 inches) deep. When its source of organic matter, the forest itself, is removed, this layer quickly erodes and disappears. After just a few growing seasons, all that remains is dry, sterile land furrowed by deep cracks.

TEMPERATE FOREST   TROPICAL FOREST

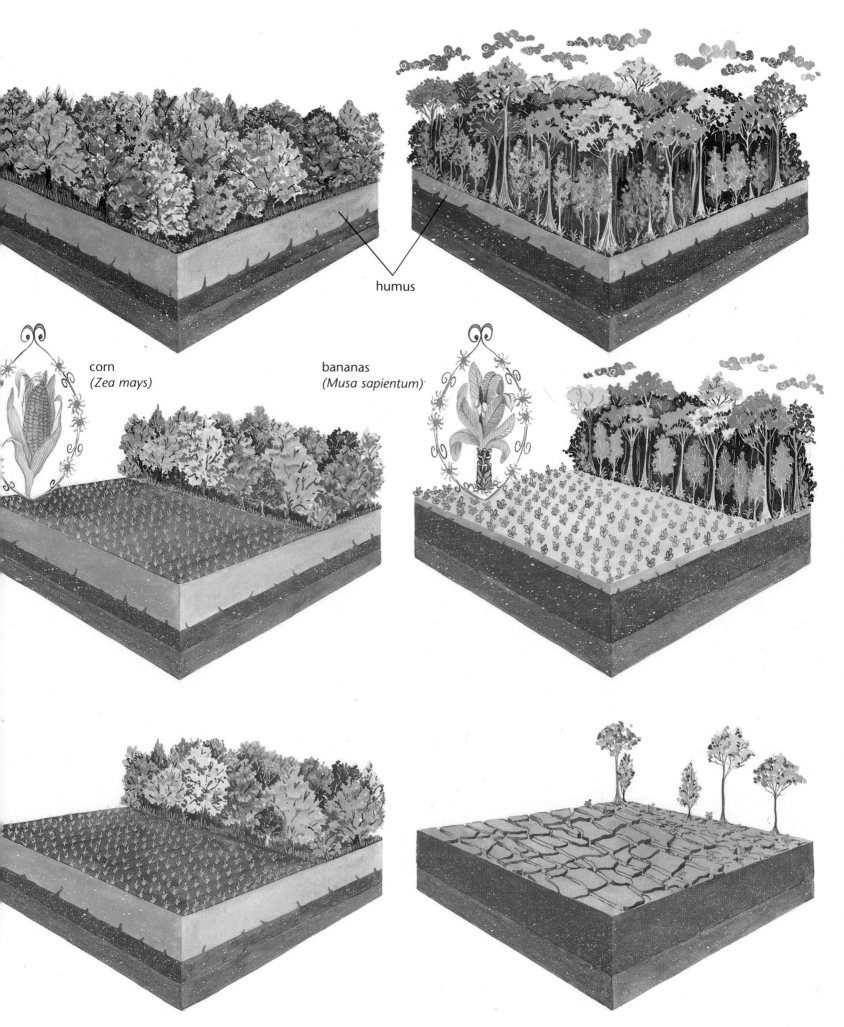

humus

corn
(Zea mays)

bananas
(Musa sapientum)

15

TYPES OF TROPICAL FORESTS

A Wall of Plants

When you fly over the Amazon basin, Borneo, or New Guinea, the forest looks like a uniform **canopy** of treetops. There are many shades of green but few other colors. The only breaks in the green canopy are the sparkling rivers snaking lazily through the landscape. If you take a boat along one of these rivers, you will see little more. Walls of plants rise from both banks and are draped with a dense curtain of **lianas** and **aerial roots**. But the vast vegetation is not as uniform as it appears. The composition and structure of the forest change in relation to its geographical location. Changes also occur in relation to altitude, soil types, and local climate. There are three basic types of tropical forests: the lowland rain forest, the monsoon forest, and the mountain forest.

Lowland Rain Forests

In lowland rain forests, most vegetation consists of trees and shrubs. There are few herbaceous plants. The trees are mostly **evergreens**. On average, they reach heights between 30 and 35 meters (98 and 115 feet). Isolated trees may reach as high as 60 to 70 meters (197 to 230 feet). Below this green canopy is a third tree level that grows to heights between 10 and 30 meters (33 and 98 feet). These trees have a very vertical structure, so they can make the best use of all the available space. Lower down, saplings and shrubs struggle to grow and adapt to the semidarkness of the forest floor. They are ready to begin a burst of rapid growth should a gap in the canopy open up and allow sunlight to shine through.

The structure of the tropical forests is further complicated by countless lianas and **epiphytes**. They are much more common here than in temperate forests. Some lianas may reach lengths of 200 meters (656 feet) and diameters of 20 centimeters (8 inches). They are most numerous in forests that have been disturbed by humans.

The three illustrations show the principal types of tropical forests.
1. The mountain forest of Borneo
2. The Indian monsoon forest. In Central America or in Africa, the seasonal characteristics may be more distinct.
3. The true rain forest
The three types of forests are often found in the same geographical area fairly close together. Some of their animal life is common to each forest type. Each type, however, is characterized by distinct temperature and rainfall patterns, by very different plant species, and by general structures.

1

2

3

17

There are various types of epiphytes: herbaceous, shrubs, or lianas. Epiphytes do not root in soil but grow on the trees in search of light.

The canopy topping the lowland forest is so dense, it blocks 99 percent of the sunlight. Only on the riverbanks and in the natural or artificial clearings do rays of sunlight reach the forest floor to enable the growth of plants in the lower layers.

Monsoon Forests

In some areas of Asia, Africa, and Central America there is a fairly long dry season. Under these conditions, the evergreen rain forest develops along streams and rivers. Elsewhere, the forest is less dense and made up of trees that lose their leaves during the dry season. A rich **undergrowth** develops in the large **clearings** of these forests along with a carpet of grass that encourages the presence of **herbivorous** mammals.

Mountain Forests

Various types of tropical mountain forests exist in almost all tropical upland areas with heights of up to 3,500 to 4,000 meters (11,483 to 13,123 feet). These forests are common in Africa on the continent's isolated mountains. They are also found in Oceania, especially in Borneo and New Guinea, and in the Americas along the entire length of the vast Andes **cordillera**.

The vegetation of the mountain forests generally becomes less dense the higher you climb. The canopy is lower, and clearings colonized by ferns open up. Still higher, the trees are covered with mosses and lichens, which hang like giant garlands from the trunks and small twisted branches. Here the sun is often hidden by clouds. The atmosphere is gray and silent, as if it were muffled by the suspended droplets of the frequent fogs.

1. A view of Mount Kinabalu in Borneo. At 4,101 meters (13,455 feet), Mount Kinabalu is the "roof" of the island. It is dominated by typical mountain vegetation that has an unusual abundance of rhododendrons, ferns, and mosses.

2. A monsoon forest in northern India. In spite of the clearly seasonal rainfall pattern, the Asian monsoon forests are still dominated by evergreens that manage to survive the dry season while retaining part of their foliage.

3. A rain forest in Queensland, Australia. The true rain forest has a more complex structure than the mountain and seasonal forests.

1

2

3

TROPICAL PLANTS

An Extraordinary Wealth of Species
If you read the classic adventure stories you might get the sense that a tropical forest is a dense jungle that you must fight your way through with a machete. That dense jungle is actually a **secondary community**. It can be compared to the **bramble thickets** that often

There is a huge range of species in this environment. No less than 110 tree species live in an area of just 1,000 square meters (10, 764 square feet) in the Manaus region of Brazil. Elsewhere in the Amazon basin, 423 trees belonging to 87 different species were counted in 10,000 square meters

a dozen tree species. Three or four of these are **dominant species**.

Problematic Pollination
The most significant consequence of this great range of species is the difficulty tropical rain forest plants have reaching and

grow in environments that are severely disturbed by roads, railroads, rivers, and the outskirts of villages. The shrubs or herbaceous plants that should grow on the forest floor struggle to grow in primary tropical rain forests because the canopy formed by the trees is so dense. It is therefore fairly easy to walk among the immense trunks.

(107,643 square feet) of land. In Brunei, on the island of Borneo, 760 tree species with trunks at least 10 centimeters (4 inches) in diameter have been identified in an area of 40 hectares (99 acres). This range of species is absolutely enormous when compared to the range of species found in **temperate forests**. In temperate forests there are at most

pollinating others of their species. Wind and insect pollination are not efficient methods in these conditions of extreme variety. For this reason, **symbiotic relationships** have developed between particular plants and **specialist** insects, **hummingbirds**, **Nectariniidae**, fruit bats, or other animals. In any case, the rain forests are dominated by **angiosperms**.

Angiosperms are the only plants equipped with pollination systems suited to the scattered and different populations of this environment.

There is one curious exception. It is a simple lianalike **gymnosperm** of the Gnetales order. This plant produces seeds in a fleshy layer about 2 millimeters (.08 inch) thick rather than the usual "naked seeds" of the gymnosperms. This fleshy layer contains a

in **temperate zones**. These traits include the form of the trunk and leaves, and the type of branching and flowers.

The trunk of a rain forest tree is usually long, straight, and slim. It branches only at the very top. At the base, the trunk expands into **buttresses**, or winged ribs, that look like huge feet. They may also be caged by natural supports, such as the aerial roots of the *Ficus*.

family and the Ciperaceae family. In temperate regions, species from these families always have long, narrow leaves.

The flowers of the rain forest trees often grow directly on the main branches or trunks. This arrangement makes them more accessible to many animals that would not normally climb as high as the canopy. The intermediate layers of the forest are occupied by many epiphytes and lianas. These plants help to create various specialized environments populated by insects, spiders, and small **vertebrates** of all kinds.

0

13

1

14

2

15

The photos here show a number of tropical plants.
1. *Strelitzia nicolai* **2.** Orchid *Cymbidium* genus **3.** Orchid *Oncidium* genus
4. *Anthurium andraeanum* **5.** Orchid *Phalaenopsis amabilis* **6.** *Aloe striata* flower
7. *Calathea setosa* **8.** Orchid *Phalaenopsis* genus **9.** *Ficus* genus **10.** *Mahonia comarifolia* **11.** Lily **12.** *Melaleuca cypericifolia* flower **13.** Bamboo
14. Bamboo stem **15.** *Cycas revoluta* palm

sugary juice and is a **false fruit**. The seeds are dispersed far from the parent plant after they have been eaten by **toucans** and passed through their intestines.

Unusual Characteristics
Many rain forest trees have traits that distinguish them from the usual tree forms found

The leaves of the rain forest trees are usually large, with full **laminae**, or blades. They are oblong or **elliptical** in shape, often having a tapering point that allows water to run off easily. This form of leaf is so functional that it is also common on the herbaceous plants of the forest undergrowth. It is also seen among the grasses of the Gramineae

Pages 22–23:
An imaginary tropical forest that could easily be constructed by relocating tropical forest plants from various parts of the world on their original levels.

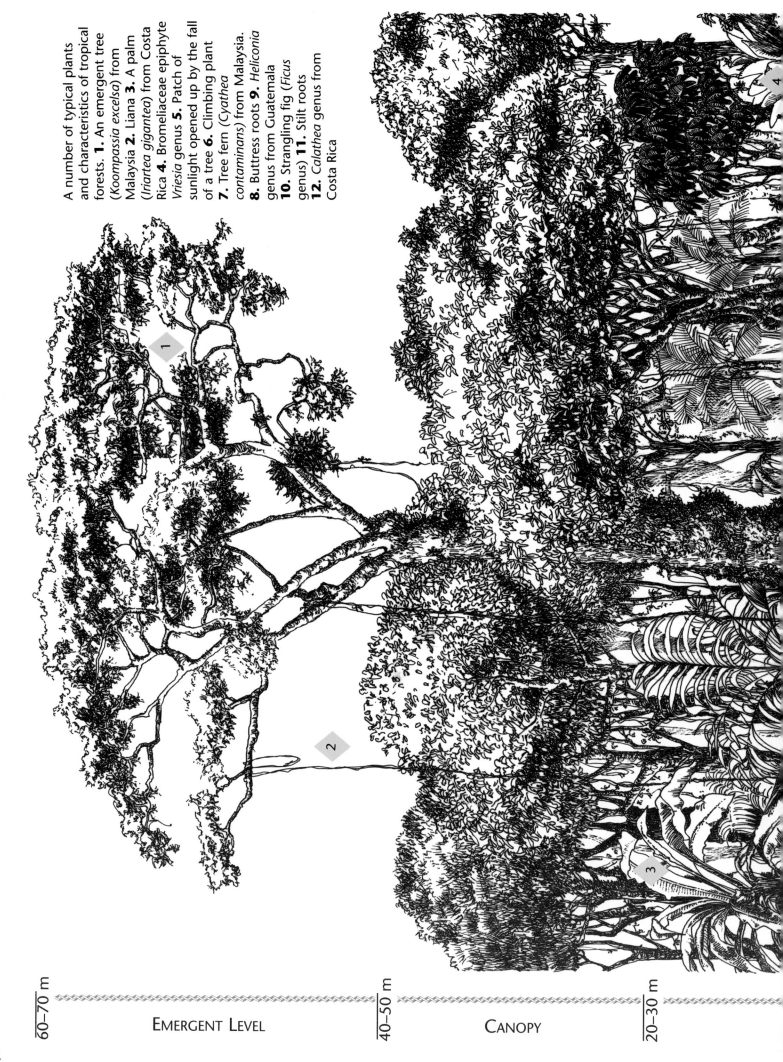

A number of typical plants and characteristics of tropical forests. **1.** An emergent tree (*Koompassia excelsa*) from Malaysia **2.** Liana **3.** A palm (*Iriartea gigantea*) from Costa Rica **4.** Bromeliaceae epiphyte *Vriesia* genus **5.** Patch of sunlight opened up by the fall of a tree **6.** Climbing plant **7.** Tree fern (*Cyathea contaminans*) from Malaysia. **8.** Buttress roots **9.** *Heliconia* genus from Guatemala **10.** Strangling fig (*Ficus* genus) **11.** Stilt roots **12.** *Calathea* genus from Costa Rica

60–70 m

40–50 m

20–30 m

EMERGENT LEVEL

CANOPY

THE FOREST ANIMALS

A Day at Klong-Nakah

A walk along the edge of a tropical forest offers visitors an endless display of life in motion. Imagine taking a brief morning walk in the area around the small human settlement at the Klong-Nakah forest station in southern Thailand.

A **drongo cuckoo** (*Surniculus lugubris*) suns itself on the grass in front of the foresters' huts. A small crested lizard (*Calotes* genus) scampers up a tree trunk. At the top of a tree sits a three-striped sparrow hawk (*Accipiter trivirgatus*). From the thick of the forest comes the trilling of a **shama** (*Copsychus malabaricus*) and the cries of an oriole (*Oriolus chinensis*).

As you enter the forest and immerse yourself in the deep shadows, you hear the constant chirping of the countless crickets. The repeated cries of the **gibbons** (*Hylobates lar*) calling to each other echo in the distance. Suddenly you catch a glimpse of a red-bellied squirrel (*Callosciurus ferrugineus*) climbing nimbly in a bamboo thicket followed by a yellow-throated marten (*Martes flavigula*). Both animals disappear into the tree canopy.

Above the river is a broad ribbon of sky. You spot a sea eagle (*Haliaeetus* genus) with a white breast that disappears suddenly as it glides along the water. Shortly afterward, two **great hornbills** (*Buceros bicornis*) make their appearance high in the sky. Their cries vaguely resemble those of a raven.

Tree-dwelling Animals

Some people believe tropical forests are very secretive and unrewarding places. This is only partly true. They are certainly secretive. For each animal you see or hear, there are another hundred or thousand that pass by unobserved. However, tropical forests are anything but unrewarding. You can walk for hours without seeing two examples of the same species. The tropical forest is so diverse it offers a thousand different pictures of itself that are rarely repeated.

The animals living in tropical forests share certain characteristics. For example, the ability to hang from the trees is clearly important in a multilayered forest ecosystem. Being able to hang in some way makes an animal open to attack by **predators**. Many birds, such as orioles, flycatchers, and tree-creepers, build hanging nests, as do some wasps. The cocoons of many moths and wasps hang from the branches on fine threads. By hanging their webs in places that are hard to reach, spiders are able to avoid the attacks of their main predators, the army ants.

Many animals have evolved into tree-dwellers even though their close relatives in other areas of the world live on the ground. The special traits of such animals include a fairly light weight, **opposable thumbs**, and **prehensile tails**. Among these specialized animals are the remarkable South American sloths, the tree-dwelling anteaters, many snakes, lizards, and frogs, and both **Old World** and **New World** monkeys.

Many birds live in the trees, using natural cavities or digging their own in which to safely nest. The nests help the birds avoid attacks from predators and possible floods. Among these birds are the Afro-Asian hornbills, the South American toucans and **motmots**, the African **hoopoes**, and the parrots, **quetzals**, and woodpeckers found in all tropical zones.

Army Ants and Poisonous Frogs

Among the countless species of insects in tropical forests, the ants and **termites** are certainly noticeable. Two of the best known are the army ants and the leafcutter ants of the Amazon. Termite nests are found in all vegetation levels. The wood-eating termites make a great contribution to the decomposition of woody plant tissues.

The high humidity levels present in tropical forests make them suitable for **amphibians**. These animals often live out of the water on the branches of the trees or among the damp leaves on the forest floor. They include many brightly colored species, like the Amazonian *Dendrobates* frogs. The bright colors are warnings that the skins of these frogs are very poisonous.

Constant high temperatures favor the presence of **invertebrates** and reptiles. In the Amazon forest, you can find spiders that are large enough to capture and eat small birds that become trapped in their webs. Some moths have wingspans that are up to 30 centimeters (12 inches). A millipede may be as long as 28 centimeters (11 inches). Some snails are 20 centimeters (8 inches) long. Among the snakes, the **pythons**, **boas**, and **anacondas** may exceed 6 or 7 meters (20 or 23 feet) in length.

Many animals act as pollinators. Many more, including birds and fruit-eating mammals, like fruit bats and monkeys, are responsible for **dispersing** seeds.

Animals can reproduce at any time in the tropical forests, where rainfall and temperature are relatively constant throughout the year. However, many species restrict reproduction to certain periods in which the resources they need are particularly abundant. This phenomenon becomes more common as you move from the equator toward the tropics.

1. A view of an Asian lowland tropical rain forest with four of its most typical large animals.
2. Rhinoceros hornbill (*Buceros rhinoceros*). The hornbills form a large family of very similar birds commonly found in tropical Asia, with one species being found as far away as New Guinea, and Africa.
3. Tiger (*Panthera tigris*). The tiger is a large Asian carnivore that also lives in the northern forests of the continent, including the famous Siberian tiger of which only a few dozen examples survive.
4. Gray-headed sea eagle (*Icthyophaga ichthyaetus*). A bird of prey native to tropical Asia.
5. Crested langur (*Presbytis cristatus*). The entire langur group is found only in tropical Asia.

2

3

4

5

AFRICA

African and South American tropical forest environments with some of their most typical large animals.

1. The illustration of the African forest shows from left to right: the okapi *(Okapia johnstoni)*, a large Giraffidae only discovered early this century in Zaire. Above the okapi, a green touraco, *(Tauraco persa)*. Center: a rusty colobus

2

3

SOUTH AMERICA

(*Colobus badius ferrugineus*), a typical tree-dwelling monkey from the lowland forests. Bottom right: a Congo peafowl (*Afropavo congensis*). On the tree trunk, right: two pangolins (*Manis tricuspis*).

2. A wooden baboon mask from Zaire

3. A wooden mask from Nigeria portraying an imaginary horned crocodile

4. The illustration of the South American forest shows, from left to right: a green-winged macaw (*Ara chloroptera*) in flight, one of the largest parrots. Below the macaw, on the ground: a striped basilisk (*Basiliscus vittatus*), a tree-dwelling lizard. A toucan (*Ramphastos sulfuratus*) with its enormous multicolored beak. A margay (*Felis wiedii*), a big cat similar to the ocelot. Hanging from a branch, a three-toed sloth (*Bradypus tridactylus*), a mammal perfectly adapted to life in the trees.

5. A quetzal (*Pharomachrus mocinno*), a magnificent bird depicted in Aztec mythology and symbolic of Guatemala.

4

The head of a jaguar
(Panthera onca) set against a
backdrop showing the tropical
forests of the Americas, where this
great predator can be found.

THE MONKEYS

Tree-dwelling Mammals
One of the many fascinating features of the tropical forests is that they are the environment of choice for most **primates**, the order of mammals to which humans belong. With the exception of the **Barbary ape** and the **Japanese macaque**, the primates live between 30 degrees north and 30 degrees south latitude, within the tropics. A few primates, such as **baboons, hamadryases,** and similar species, have adapted to life on the ground in fairly open areas. Most, however, are tree-dwellers. The most important factors that have influenced the **evolution** of the primates and affected their physical structure result from the fact that they live in trees.

From Lemurs to Catarrhines
The oldest primates, the **lemurs,** have eyes that point forward and flat nails instead of claws. They have an excellent sense of smell, indicated by their large whiskers and damp noses, and they eat insects and small vertebrates. Lemurs, which are related to monkeys, are **nocturnal,** which means they are active during the night. Monkeys have a **diurnal** life, which means they are most active during the day.

Compared to the lemurs, the monkeys' sense of smell is less developed. Their sight is better in relation to calculating distances in three dimensions when making long and dangerous leaps. Their fingers are good at gripping, and their thumbs are fully opposable, which means they can be pressed up against the other fingers. The eyes of the true monkeys are set in the front of the head, are larger in size, and for the first time among the mammals, are capable of color vision. Color vision is useful for distinguishing food and predators in an environment dominated by green.

NON-BRACHIATING

Two non-brachiating monkeys: **1.** The Asian langur (*Presbytis entellus*) of the catarrhine family **2.** The South American squirrel monkey (*Saimiri sciurea*) of the platyrrhine family. Note the movement similar to other tree-dwelling mammals such as squirrels.

BRACHIATING

Two brachiating catarrhine monkeys from tropical Asia: **3.** A gibbon (*Hylobates lar*) **4.** An orangutan (*Pongo pygmaeus*).

These monkeys are defined as anthropoids because as they increased in size, they had to adopt a new type of movement. Natural selection led to a "humanoid" type of body structure. This new structure was to be crucial in the adoption of an erect stance when, around 10 million years ago, circumstances forced some of these unusual primates to live on the ground.

The monkeys can be divided into two large groups: the New World monkeys, or **platyrrhines**, and the Old World monkeys, or **catarrhines**. The New World monkeys have flat noses, prehensile tails, and jaws similar to those of the lemurs. They usually have 36 teeth. The Old World monkeys have prominent noses. Very few have prehensile tails. They often have very small tails or no tail at all and specialized jaws with 32 teeth. New World monkeys include the monkeys from Central and South America, such as the **marmosets**, a group of small species. The Old World monkeys include the Asian and African monkeys, such as the **anthropoids**, a small group of primates to which the human species belongs.

Brachiation and the Origins of Humans
The key to human origins lies in the gradual increase in size of certain tree-dwelling anthropoids. This occurred around 20 million years ago with the evolution of *Dryopithecus*. In South America, the monkeys adapted perfectly to life in the trees. They developed prehensile tails, and some species decreased in size and became able to move as quickly and as easily as squirrels.

In the Old World, some tree-dwelling monkeys became so large that they were forced to move along the branches by hanging by their arms, a movement known as **brachiating**, instead of leaping from one branch to the next. The evolutionary effects of this change of position were the loss of the tail and the adjustment of the entire body to the new hanging or "pre-erect" position. The monkeys' tails helped them when they leapt from branch to branch but were a handicap to monkeys moving by brachiating.

When the great African tropical forests retreated and the **savanna** environment

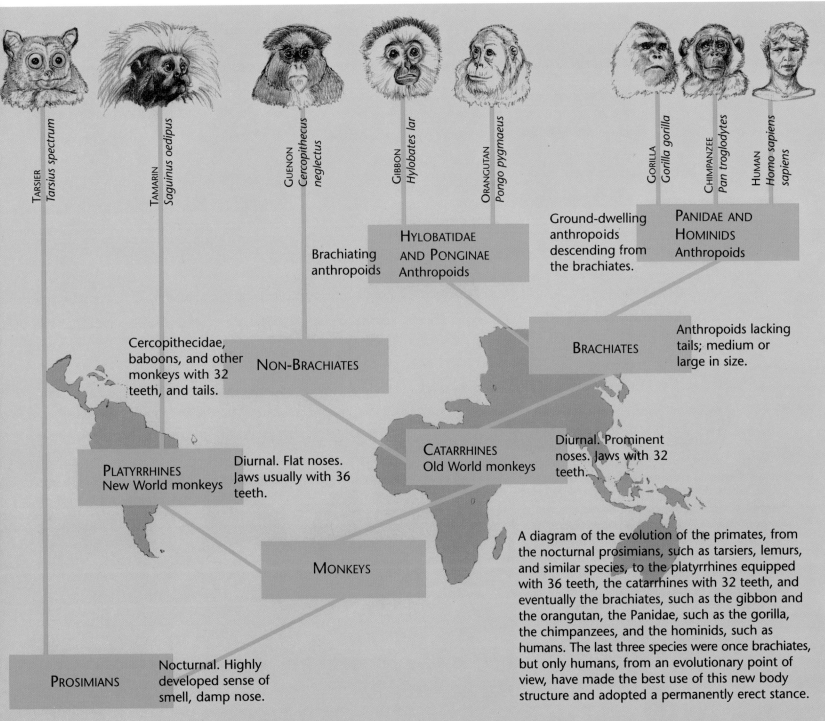

A diagram of the evolution of the primates, from the nocturnal prosimians, such as tarsiers, lemurs, and similar species, to the platyrrhines equipped with 36 teeth, the catarrhines with 32 teeth, and eventually the brachiates, such as the gibbon and the orangutan, the Panidae, such as the gorilla, the chimpanzees, and the hominids, such as humans. The last three species were once brachiates, but only humans, from an evolutionary point of view, have made the best use of this new body structure and adopted a permanently erect stance.

developed, some brachiating monkeys, such as *Ramapithecus*, who lived 14 million years ago, were forced to live on the ground, where they began to move on just two legs. This begins the long story of the origins of humans. This story unfolded in the savanna over the last 10 million years but would not have been possible without the brachiation phase in the tropical forest. The proof is provided by the baboons, African monkeys adapted to life in the savanna that never went through a brachiating phase. The result of this evolutionary process is an intelligent and social monkey that is strictly four-legged. The baboon is far removed from the intellectual refinement of an anthropoid monkey.

The anthropoids that still live in the tropical forests are the Asian gibbons and **orangutans**. The chimpanzees and gorillas live in Africa. The Asian species are still brachiating tree-dwellers. The African species have adapted to life on the ground, although they are skillful climbers. The chimpanzees and gorillas are divided from humans by no more than 6 to 7 million years of evolution along a different path.

Illustrated against the black background are three prosimians, all from Madagascar.
1. Black-headed lemurs *(Lemur fulvus)*
2. Ring-tailed lemurs *(Lemur catta)*
3. Verreaux's sifakas *(Propithecus verreauxi)* of the Indridae family. Against the white background are two monkeys: **4.** The bald ouakari *(Cacajao calvo)*, a South American platyrrhine **5.** An African baboon *(Papio cynocephalus)*, a fairly typical representative of the catarrhine group.
In general the prosimians are nocturnal animals like the prehistoric mammals, while the monkeys are active during the day. However, the Indridae differ from the lemurs because they are actually diurnal and represent an advanced form of prosimian. Among the true monkeys, there is a nocturnal species, the douroucouli *(Aotes trivirgatus)*, another South American platyrrhine.

32

1

2

4

3

5

THE PARROTS

2. One of the most notable characteristics of the parrots is their marked sociability and the strong pair-bonding found in most known species. The male and female frequently stroke each other, an action that strengthens the bond between them.

"Three-Handed" Birds

The primates evolved within the class of mammals as a tree-dwelling highly social group capable of using its hands. The birds of the Psittacidae family, better known as parrots, evolved in a similar way. There are more than 300 parrot species. They live in the hot regions of all the continents. Parrots are perfectly adapted to life in the forests.

The main characteristic of the parrots is their powerful pincerlike bill. The bill shows that they have adapted to a very specific way of life. All the birds in the Psittacidae family, which includes all parrot species, can move their upper jaw, which is located directly on the **frontal bone**. In almost all other vertebrates, including humans, the upper jaw is fixed and cannot be moved. The parrots' lower jaw is shaped like a small shell. It can be moved both vertically, like all other birds, and laterally, or from side to side. A bill of this kind is suited to snapping, digging, and shelling large seeds. The bill can also be used as a hook to anchor the bird to a support while it is climbing.

Adaptation to life in trees led some **naturalists** of the past to draw parallels between parrots and monkeys. In both groups, the need to move through the trees has led to the development of the animals' ability to grip with their feet. Parrots and monkeys can grip supports, food, and any other objects they need to handle. Like monkeys, parrots have developed prehensile limbs that are suited to both movement and feeding. The parrots' bill has helped their adaptation because it is used as a climbing aid, allowing the bird to use its feet as hands. So, while monkeys can be considered "four-handed," parrots are "three-handed."

It is clear that in such a large group the degree of adaptation to life in the trees varies. After having conquered the trees, some species became increasingly specialized to life in this type of environment. Other species became gradually less specialized. Broadly speaking, the most typical models of the first group are the forest parrots, such as Amazons, members of the genus *Pionites*, **gray parrots**, and various short-tailed parrots. The second group includes the long-tailed parakeets of the savanna and the prairie, such as **budgerigars**, collared parakeets, and **rossellas**, which can fly much better and are more at home walking on the ground.

The Language of the Parrots

Parrots are generally very social birds and are strictly **monogamous**. In many species the male and female pair remain together all their lives. They unite not only on the raising of their young but also in the search for food and the signaling of potential danger.

This tendency to act as a couple and a group is reflected in the parrots' exceptional vocal abilities. They are capable of making different sounds to signal different situations. This ability makes it possible to train some species of parrots to talk once they are domesticated. The bird eventually considers the person taking care of it to be a member of its group. The parrot adapts itself to the sounds used by its new group member and faithfully imitates the human voice. The various words it learns are linked to different situations. It is not, therefore, true that talking parrots do not understand anything of what they say. They are perfectly capable of linking sounds and situations and are able to repeat the right words at the right moment. This has been confirmed by the recent research of American scientist Irene Pepperberg on the gray parrot. However, tales have been told about gray parrots and other parrots for many years: they bark at dogs, meow at cats, announce visitors with a "Good morning" or "Someone's here," and

1. A scarlet macaw (*Ara macao*), one of the largest and most brightly colored parrots. Parrots are very old species, directly descending from prehistoric tree-dwelling birds of which no trace remains.

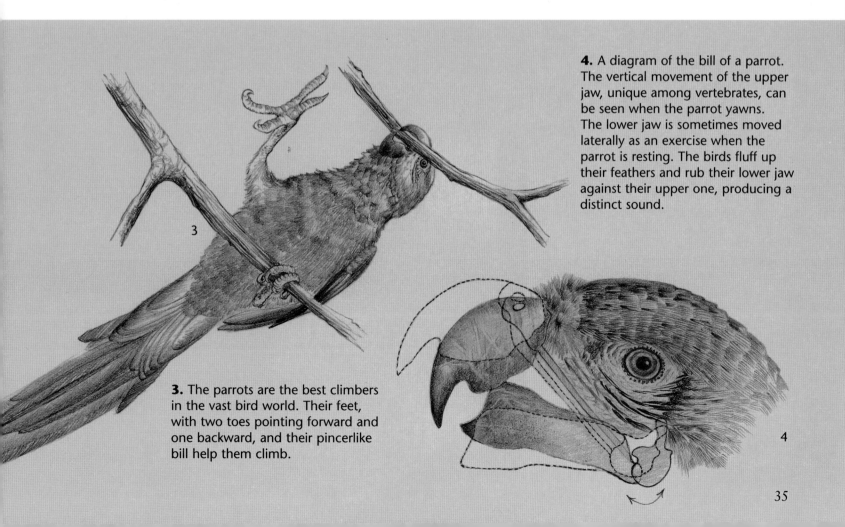

4. A diagram of the bill of a parrot. The vertical movement of the upper jaw, unique among vertebrates, can be seen when the parrot yawns. The lower jaw is sometimes moved laterally as an exercise when the parrot is resting. The birds fluff up their feathers and rub their lower jaw against their upper one, producing a distinct sound.

3. The parrots are the best climbers in the vast bird world. Their feet, with two toes pointing forward and one backward, and their pincerlike bill help them climb.

4

say "Hello" when the telephone rings.

Until very recently, naturalists believed that parrots in the wild do not imitate sounds of any kind. It was only in 1992 that three French **ornithologists** working in Zaire succeeded in recording the calls of a pair of gray parrots that included almost perfect imitations of the calls of various local bird species. It is now clear that the parrots' habit of imitation is not something that has been provoked by **captivity**. It is a natural talent, which, in all probability, has an adaptive function and is an indication of a very complex and highly evolved social system. New and fascinating questions are being posed, but there is still much work to be done before these questions can be answered with any reasonable degree of certainty.

A scarlet macaw *(Ara macao)* perched on a branch. Page 37: A hyacinth macaw *(Anodorhynchus hyacinthinus)* emerging from a hole in a tree trunk where it has built its nest. It should be noted that the principal cause of the decline of these birds is not their capture for use as domestic pets but rather the destruction of the tropical forests, the natural habitat of many of the most beautiful species. Fewer than 2,000 examples of the hyacinth macaw survive today. There are fewer than 50 Lear's macaws. The Spix's macaw is extinct in the wild, with just a few examples remaining in captivity.

THE FOREST PEOPLE

Naturalists of the Tropical Rain Forest
The tropical rain forest may appear to be unfriendly to humans. It is, however, an environment rich in resources. These resources allow for the existence of a large number of living things. It was unavoidable that people who reached the edges of the tropical forest tried to use this wealth of resources. There are forest-dwelling populations on all the continents that have learned to use the tropical forests, while neither destroying them nor exhausting them. These populations include the Pygmies in Africa, the Dayaks in Borneo, the Papua in New Guinea, and the various Amerindian groups in the Amazon basin.

As the French naturalist Jean Dorst writes: "It is right to highlight the harmonious relationship of the Indians with the immense Amazon forest of which they know all the resources, judiciously classified according to a tradition handed down from father to son. The trees and even the smallest animals have a name… and the people know how they live, where to find them, and how to use them. Except for the Pygmies of Central Africa and certain ethnic groups of the Indo-Pacific region, there are no better naturalists than the Indians of the Amazon. Even today biologists still benefit from their knowledge."

a. The location of a number of Amerindian groups particularly well adapted to life in the tropical forests:
1. Amerindian groups from the Venezuelan interior
2. Amazon hunters
3. Pygmies
4. Southeast Asian hunters
5. Negritos from Malaysia
6. Hunters from Borneo

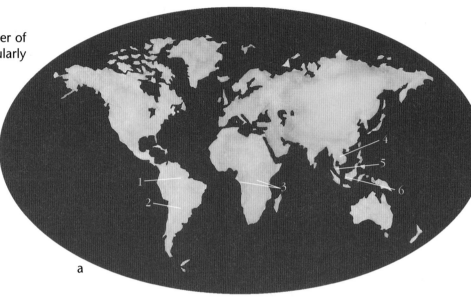

a

b. The phenomenon of the reduced dimensions of the forest mammals compared with those of the savanna can be seen in different populations of the same species, such as elephants, buffalo, and humans, or between two related species, such as hippopotamuses, giraffes, antelope, and chimpanzees.

b

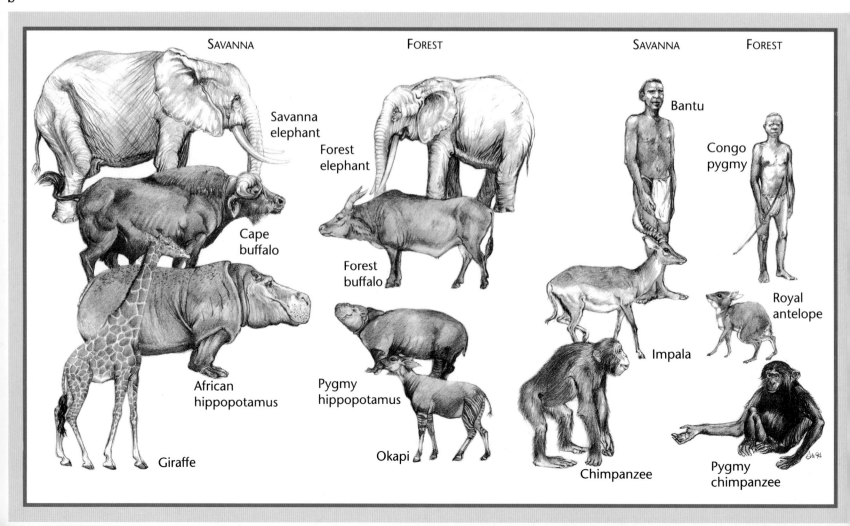

SAVANNA FOREST SAVANNA FOREST

Savanna elephant
Forest elephant
Cape buffalo
Forest buffalo
African hippopotamus
Pygmy hippopotamus
Giraffe
Okapi
Bantu
Congo pygmy
Royal antelope
Impala
Chimpanzee
Pygmy chimpanzee

The skill with which forest people identify living things using all their senses is truly extraordinary. Faced with a tree whose lowest leaves are 25 to 30 meters (82 to 98 feet) overhead, a Pygmy from Central Africa will first carefully examine the bark, perhaps cutting away a piece to expose the underlying wood. He or she will observe its color, smell it, slowly chew it, and then arrive at its exact classification. Some years ago, the American ornithologist Jared Diamond decided to study the names of the birds used by a Papua tribe. He found that almost all the species, even those of no economic value, had a name in the local language. The only exception was shown by two species so alike they were indistinguishable to anyone but an expert in the field.

Perfect Adaptation to the Environment

This amazing skill of peoples living in tropical forest regions has distant origins. People of the rain forests, such as the Papua of New Guinea, the Pygmies of Africa, or the Yanomani of the Amazon, made their way into the jungle thousands of years ago to escape competition with more competitive populations that occupied all the available open spaces. The return to the forest environment, which the ancestors of humans had left millions of years ago, was followed by a number of physical **adaptations** that occurred in parallel in many different populations. The most observable adaptation is the reduction in average size of the individual members of the population. This is also a characteristic of forest animals. There are forest-dwelling buffalo, elephants, deer, and pigs, and in each species or family the adaptation to the forest environment has led to a reduction in size. This is clearly an advantage when moving through the tree trunks and branches.

Cultures Threatened with Extinction

The forest people gather wild fruits and hunt and fish. They use simple weapons like bows and arrows and sometimes powerful poisons obtained from certain plants or animals. All these adaptations and all the culture accumulated and preserved over thousands of years have not prevented the decline in population of these people. Today, in a period of unparalleled destruction of the tropical forests, they risk disappearing altogether. In every area of the world, people adapted for life in the forest are found. Terrible stories of invasion, violence, slavery, epidemics, and assassinations are also found. In Brazil, in Indonesia, in Borneo and in many other places, the human occupants of the forests are victims. They are living witnesses to the horrors arising from the desire of the strong to obtain resources from the weak with no regard for their needs.

c. A scene of everyday life in an Amazon village. The huts have been built in a clearing on the riverbank. The women are performing the domestic tasks while the men search the riverbanks or leave the village in a dugout canoe to hunt or fish.

1. A Baka pygmy settlement in a Cameroon forest
2. An Orang Asli village on the Malay peninsula
3. Yanomani women and children resting in a hut in their village in the Amazon basin. Throughout the world, the culture of people of the tropical forests is based on small-scale nomadic agriculture as well as on hunting and gathering. The clearings they open in the vegetation are small enough to be easily recolonized by the trees when the small community moves on.

3

DEFORESTATION AND MASS EXTINCTION

The Same Fate as the Dinosaurs

The two most direct, tragic, and dramatic results of the destruction of the tropical forests are the disappearance of the ancient human forest cultures, and often the people themselves, and the mass extinction of a great number of animal and plant species. The second result is less alarming to people, but it is of great importance to the immediate future of our planet.

Of the 5 to 30 million living species, many thousands disappear each year. The total number of species is a very inexact estimate, and the majority of species are tiny invertebrates found in very restricted areas. Just a few centuries ago, an average of one species became extinct each year. The extinction of species is a natural event. However, the speed with which extinction occurs increases greatly during certain periods of crisis. A crisis occurred at the end of the Cretaceous period, 65 million years ago, when the dinosaurs, the **ammonites**, and many other groups of animals and plants became extinct. For the first time since that period, a huge number of species are heading for extinction. The phenomenon is clearly linked to widespread environmental destruction that is underway, especially **deforestation**.

Among the vertebrates, there are thousands of animals on the endangered species list. The experts judge these species to be in danger of complete extinction. One thousand of the nine thousand species of birds are endangered. If this ratio of 1:9 between endangered and existing species is applied to all living things, a reasonably accurate projection, over the next 30 or 40 years our planet could lose between one and five million species.

Disastrous Fragmentation

Even though what remains of the tropical forests covers only 6 percent of the Earth's dry land, which is about one-third of their original size, they house about 50 percent of the planet's plant and animal species. Separated by great rivers and vast mountain ranges, tropical forests represent unique and irreplaceable environments.

The idea that people can conserve a fairly complete sample while reducing the tropical forests to one-tenth their current size is both wishful and misleading. Many small species would be brushed aside with their entire natural **habitat**. Other large species would fail to adapt to the fragmentation, or breaking up, of their ancient habitats. The theory of so-called **insular biogeography** that was developed around 20 years ago by the biologists John MacArthur and Edward O. Wilson clearly shows that the processes of extinction are closely linked to those of habitat fragmentation.

Unstoppable Devastation

The destruction of the tropical forests is now so vast and widespread, it would be almost impossible to stop without reversing the processes currently taking place. According to Norman Myers, one of the world's chief experts on this subject, the rate of deforestation increased from 75,000 square kilometers (28,960 square miles) per year in 1979 to 142,000 square kilometers (54,830 square miles) in 1989. It is currently growing at a rate of 169,000 square kilometers (65,256 square miles) per year. A reversal of this line of development would require huge investment in favor of a rapid decrease in the human birthrate in developing countries and a limit on industrial production in developed countries. Unfortunately, there is no sign in wealthy countries of the political will needed to make the needed investments for these goals to be reached.

Given this situation, the destruction of the tropical forests will continue to be the main cause of the extinction of species over the coming years. Any conservation efforts directed elsewhere, for example, against hunting, poaching, or the trade in animals and plants, will be in vain. They may even make matters worse due to the drain on economic and human resources and the raising of false hopes.

A road under construction in the Amazon forest. The range of economic and social causes of the destruction of the tropical forests is very different in the various continents where this phenomenon is taking place. In Africa and Asia, trees are felled for their wood, which is sold abroad and replaced by plantations of various types. In South America, forest destruction is frequently caused by governments making way for the foundation of new cities in remote zones. These cities are then linked to the rest of the country by great roads, such as the one shown here in Brazil. Thousands of fires are lit along the road to strip the land of all vegetation.

© Mireille VAUTIER
BRAZIL

CARAJAS MINING PROJ.
PARA STATE BRAZIL

A gold mine opened in the "Grande Caracas" project in the state of Para in Brazil. This project, which has been underway for more than ten years, involves an area of the Brazilian Amazon covering around 1 million square kilometers (386,130 square miles). The project calls for plans to dedicate vast areas to agriculture, livestock farming, and the production of wood, as well as the construction of new mines, railroads, roads, and hydroelectric projects.

An oil well near Accedas in Peru. These sites may appear modest when compared to the vast areas destined for agriculture, but the destruction they cause is multiplied along the roads that were opened up in the forest to get to the site.

GRANATA
PRESS
SERVICE
s.d.

A fire in the Amazon forest. On September 9, 1987, the American meteorological satellites *NOAA-9* and *NOAA-10* recorded a total of 7,603 fires in the Amazon basin. On that occasion, experts cautiously calculated that in that year no less than 170,000 fires were raised in the Amazon basin resulting in the destruction of about 77,000 square meters (828,848 square feet) of forest. A great many fires were concentrated along the new roads. In some cases, it was proven that the fires were lit by colonists following the road builders in order to occupy the areas of forest along the route followed by the roads.

AMAZON rain forest

Zebu grazing on land deforested by burning in the Amazon basin. In many South American countries, beef production has increased three- or even four-fold between 1960 and 1980. However, the low price of beef produced in South America does not reflect the efficiency of its production methods but rather the effects of a policy of encouraging development. In many countries, livestock farmers obtain their land almost free of charge and take advantage of generous tax benefits given because they help to "release" the forest from its "unproductive" natural state. Under these conditions, even the production of 20 to 100 head of cattle per 250 acres, rather than the 300 to 500 head of cattle produced on a similar area in North America or Europe, is good business.

47

ALTERNATIVES TO DESTRUCTION

Economic Pressures

It is vital that every effort made to resist the forces responsible for the reduction of **biodiversity** on our planet is focused on the destruction of habitats. Programs currently being sponsored by charities and environmental groups assume that the destruction of habitat in developing nations is caused by ignorance. In order to combat this ignorance, great importance is placed on environmental education and the establishment and promotion of environmental organizations in Africa, Asia, and South America.

There is, however, a completely different point of view expressed by American zoologist Michael Robinson in a recent book on biodiversity. According to this view, environmental destruction currently taking place has nothing to do with ignorance. It is the result of economic pressures. Given the current distribution of wealth, **developing countries** in which most of the tropical forests are to be found are required to use their natural resources to try to improve their economic position and to obtain the funds needed to buy goods made abroad. So, if we are going to stop the destruction, it is of no use founding new branches of environmental groups in developing countries. Instead, we need to find other means of producing **subsistent** goods, such as food, fuel, and construction materials, and consumer goods that avoid destroying the environment.

Alternative Meats

Some likely alternatives have come from basic studies of a number of forest animals, such as the **iguana** (*Iguana iguana*), a tree-dwelling lizard of Central and South America, and the **paca** (*Cuniculus paca*), a rodent similar to a large guinea pig that lives on the forest floor in South America. Both species have very nutritious meat with excellent flavor and are typically eaten in South America.

Studies of the iguana carried out in Panama with the support of the Smithsonian Tropical Research Institute have shown that large numbers of this animal can easily be raised by gathering the eggs and raising the young in captivity for the first year of their lives. In this way, the percentage of eggs that hatches is increased from 50 percent to 95 percent. The percentage of young iguanas surviving the first year of life is also increased from 5 percent to 100 percent. The young iguana can then be released into the wild. After three years, the iguana can be captured

again. Iguanas provide a **sustainable** annual crop of 93 kilograms (205 pounds) of meat per acre compared to the 6 kilograms (13 pounds) per acre of beef obtained from the poor pastures of the deforested land. However, like the paca or other animals, such as the **bearded pig** (*Sus barbatus*) from Borneo, Java, and the Philippines, the iguana has an enormous advantage over beef cattle: the forest is not destroyed to farm these animals but is actually restored.

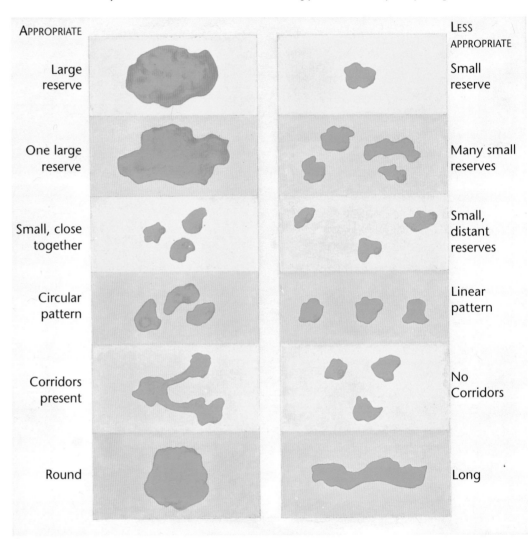

Other Options for Preserving the Rain Forests

Another research project sponsored by the Smithsonian Tropical Research Institute is concerned with choosing and distributing species of plants that can enrich the soil as well as be used as food, animal feed, fuel, or timber. The best results have been obtained with a number of **tubers** (*Marata arundinacea, Dioscorea bulbifera*), **legumes** (*Gliricidia saepium, Erythrina* genus), wild

bananas (*Musa* genus), a palm (*Bactris gasipaes*), and others.

Elsewhere efforts are being made to develop methods that allow natural products of the forest to be used without destroying the environment. There are problems, however, because the selective logging of valuable trees is often difficult. The forest may also be very sensitive to ecological disturbance. A great number of species may be lost even when the canopy is thinned by only 10 percent.

The extremely complicated ecological links within the tropical forests translate into two practical results. First, there are a number of substances that may be useful to people, such as drugs, **herbicides**, and **fungicides**, that have developed during the course of **coevolution**. Second, complicated symbiotic relationships have developed. Interference in these relationships might cause a **chain reaction** that results in extinction of an unknown number of species. For example, it has been shown that about 30 species of trees from Costa Rica reproduce with great difficulty and risk extinction. It is likely that the dispersal of the seeds of these plants was carried out by certain large fruit-eating mammals that became extinct a few hundred years ago.

The tropical forests offer immense beauty and cultural and economic wealth. It is now vital that we find sustainable ways to use these resources so that they have economic benefits. This is the only alternative to the destruction of the forests. It is an opportunity that will pass quickly, and if it is not grasped now, it may be lost forever.

1. A diagram of the standards ecologists have identified as the most appropriate for drawing the boundaries of nature reserves. The reserves are considered "islands" of habitats in territories changed by human activities.

2. A diagram drawn in 1990 by the Conservation International agency to define the most important areas for conservation in the Amazon in relation to biodiversity, the number of species in a

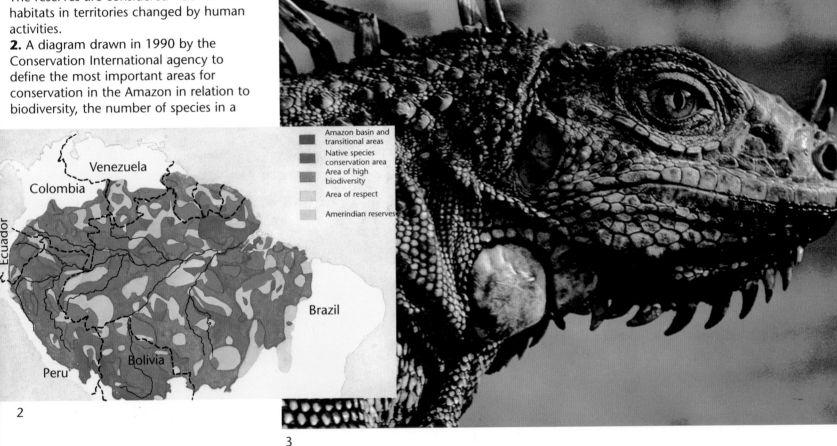

Venezuela

Colombia

Ecuador

Peru

Bolivia

Brazil

Amazon basin and transitional areas

Native species conservation area

Area of high biodiversity

Area of respect

Amerindian reserves

2

3

certain area, and the species exclusive to an area. The development plans formed on the basis of these studies should guarantee a maximum economic benefit with a minimum ecological sacrifice. Many scientists doubt a large operation of fragmentation and penetration like that planned for the Amazon can be carried out without major biological consequences.

3. The head of an iguana, a forest lizard common in Central and South America.

4. A paca, a rodent similar to a large guinea pig, common in the South American forests. Recent studies show that it makes better sense to preserve the forest, harvest the meat of wild animals, and plant products than to destroy the forest to make way for unsustainable beef farming.

4

THE DEEP GREEN PLANET

A flying saucer observing the Earth from many points—over the Amazon, Siberia, or Borneo, for example—would see a rolling sea of treetops. Forests are the central environment of our planet: the environment that dominates and persists over time following the colonization of Earth by living things. In a climate that is not too cold or dry, the end result of colonization will be a forest of some kind. Whether broadleaf deciduous or evergreen, mixed or coniferous, tropical or temperate, it will still be a forest.

The difference between town and countryside is a product of humans, and if nature was left to its own devices, the difference would disappear in a sea of trees, like the famous temples of Cambodia. Apart from the oceans, the tundra, and the deserts, the whole planet is, will be, or would be covered with forest. In a forest environment, the terrestrial ecosystems draw breath. Their continuous labors cease, and they finally rest in a stable, durable form that is resistant to change. The concept of the town and the countryside has no future, except in the hands of people who decide it on the basis of their needs. Forests are the true future of the planet. When they are felled, burned, and uprooted, it is that very future that is being destroyed.

Ecologists say that forests are climax environments. Climax environments are stable, well defined, and balanced with a wide range of species, microclimates, and subsystems. The destruction of forests means destroying something that was established and lasting, and replacing it with something new, unstable, and temporary. The destruction of even small areas of a large forest means the extermination of native species. It also means the wiping out of small worlds with unique characteristics. The destruction of the world's great forests at the current rate—150,000 square kilometers (58,000 square miles) each year—means the destruction of the planet itself. It means increasing the danger of total collapse day by day. Whatever the outcome, our planet without its forests will be a different world: one languishing in the memories of its past splendors. Let's hope that terrible day is still a long way off, and better still, that it never arrives.

RENATO MASSA

GLOSSARY

adaptation A process in which a species changes with environmental conditions

aerial root A root that obtains nutrients from the air rather than from soil

ammonite An extinct sea animal with a spiral shell

amphibian A vertebrate that spends part of its life in water and part on land

anaconda A large, nonpoisonous South American snake that coils around and crushes its victim before eating it

angiosperm A flowering plant whose seeds are formed within a special structure called an ovary, which matures to form a fruit

anthropoid A primate group to which humans, apes, and monkeys belong

baboon A ground-dwelling monkey from the African savanna

Barbary ape (*Macaca sylvanus*) A tailless monkey that lives in the forests of Morocco and Algeria

bearded pig (*Sus barbatus*) A species of wild boar from Southeast Asia, specifically Borneo, Java, and the Philippines

biodiversity The variety of species in an ecosystem

boa A large, nonpoisonous snake that lives in tropical Central and South America and kills its victim by squeezing it to death

brachiating Adapted to moving through the trees by hanging from the arms

bramble thicket A group of bushes with thorny stems that grow close together

budgerigar An Australian parakeet that is light green with black-and-yellow markings

buttresses Roots that develop out of a tree trunk above the soil and provide a supplementary support for the tree

canopy The layer of thick vegetation formed by the branches and leaves at the tops of tall trees in a forest

captivity A period of being held prisoner or under the control of another

catarrhines Old World monkeys with narrow muzzles, closely set nostrils, and 32 teeth with partially opposable thumbs

chain reaction A reaction that triggers a series of other reactions

coevolution Evolution involving changes in two or more interdependent species affecting their interaction

cordillera A system of mountain ranges

decomposer An organism that obtains its food by feeding on and breaking down animal wastes and the remains of other organisms

deforestation The large-scale clearing of trees

developing country A country having a shortage of food, few power sources, and a low economic level

disperse To scatter

diurnal Active during the day

dominant species The most common species among those present in an area

drongo cuckoo (*Surniculus lugubris*) Asian bird similar to a drongo in size, shape, and dark coloring

elliptical Having a closed curve shaped like an egg or oval with both ends alike

epiphyte A plant that lives on other plants but does not feed on them. It is equipped with air roots or puts down roots in materials that gather in cracks on the trunk of the host plant and absorbs humidity from the atmosphere

eroded Worn away

evergreen A plant whose leaves remain green all seasons of the year

evolution The gradual development of more complicated organisms from simpler ones

false fruit A fruit, such as an apple, in which the juicy flesh forms from modifications of parts of the flower other than the ovary

fertile layer Uppermost soil layer in which most nutrients are located

frontal bone A bone that forms the forehead

fungi Kingdom of single-celled and many-celled organisms that have nuclei and are unable to carry out photosynthesis. Mushrooms are fungi.

fungicide A substance that kills fungi

gibbon Ape that lives in small family groups in the tops of trees in Southeast Asia

gray parrot (*Psittacus erithacus*) A parrot species found in the African tropical forests

great hornbill (*Buceros bicornis*) A very large Asian hornbill of the rain forest that eats mostly fruit, and has a long, white tail with black bands. It frequently reaches 9.8 meters (3 feet) in length, and makes loud barking calls.

gymnosperm Plant in which the seeds are not enclosed within an ovary

habitat The particular place an organism lives

hamadryas (*Papio hamadryas*) A baboon that lives on the plains and rocky hills of Africa and southwestern Arabia. The males have a cape of long, gray hair that falls from their head and shoulders.

herbaceous Having soft, green stems

herbicide A substance that kills plants

herbivorous Any organism that feeds only on plants

hoopoe Central European bird with a crest of feathers on the top of its head, brownish-pink body, white-and-black bands on the wings and tail, and a long curved beak, which it sticks into the soil to capture crickets, beetles, and larvae

hummingbird A very small bird of the Trochilidae family that has a very slender bill for eating nectar

iguana (*Iguana iguana*) A large tree-dwelling lizard found in the tropical forests of Central and South America

inorganic Matter that lacks carbon

insular biogeography Biological discipline that studies the distribution of organisms in "islands," or fragmented habitats, in relation to their extension, the size of populations, and the distance of the "islands" from the "continent"

invertebrate An animal without a backbone

iron oxide A compound of iron, also known as rust

Japanese macaque (*Macaca fuscata*) Monkey native to the Japanese archipelago

laminae Leaf blades

legume A dry fruit that contains a number of seeds enclosed in pods

lemur The common name for a number of monkey species from Madagascar characterized by a well-developed sense of smell and nocturnal habits

liana A kind of woody vine that can be found particularly in the tropical rain forest and that roots underground

marmoset The common name for a New World monkey of the Callithricidae family that is the world's smallest living primate

monogamous Having a single mate during a lifetime

motmot A bird found in Central and South America with an unusual tail that is spread out at the tip

naturalist A student of nature

Nectariniidae A family of small, brightly colored, nectar-eating birds found in tropical Asia and Africa

New World North, Central, and South America

nitrogen A gas element that makes up 78 percent of the atmosphere and is an essential part of all living tissues

nocturnal Active at night

nutrient A chemical substance living things need for growth, energy, and repair

Old World Europe, Asia, and Africa

opposable thumbs Thumbs that work in a direction opposite that of the fingers, such as the thumbs of a human

orangutan A large ape that lives in the lowland tropical forests of Borneo and Sumatra in Asia

organic matter Substance containing carbon that is usually associated with living things

ornithologist A scientist who studies birds

paca (*Cuniculus paca*) A rodent found in the tropical forests of South America

phosphorus A nonmetallic element needed by living things

platyrrhines New World monkeys with broad noses and widely spaced nostrils, a prehensile tail, and usually 36 teeth. They include the Cebidae, the Callithricidae, and the Callimiconidae families.

pollinating Transferring pollen from the male structure of a plant to the female structure

potassium A metallic element needed for the synthesis of protein in living things

predator An animal that lives by killing and eating other animals

prehensile tail A tail that is adapted for bending and holding

primate An order of mammals with large, well-developed brains, hands with four fingers, and an opposable thumb. They tend to live in social groups.

python A large, poisonous snake that lives in the tropical rain forests of Africa, Asia, and Australia and kills its victim by squeezing it to death

quetzal (*Pharomachrus mocinno*) Common name for a species of the Trogonidae family found in Central America and characterized by the long tail and iridescent green plumage of the male

rossella An Australian parakeet that lives mostly in open forests and bramble thickets

savanna A tropical grassland that ranges in moisture from dry scrubland to wet, open woodland

secondary community The community that colonizes an area once grasses and some plant life are established

shama (*Copsychus malabaricus*) A tropical songbird of the Turdidae family found in the Asian tropical forests

sloth A type of tree-dwelling mammal that hangs from branches and eats leaves, shoots, and fruits. It includes various species found in the tropical forests from the Honduras to Argentina.

specialist An organism with a restricted food source, living in a restricted habitat, often displaying specific behavior or structural adaptations

sterile layer A soil layer that contains almost no nutrients and is unable to support the growth of plants

subsistent Necessary to support life

sustainable Allowing for the use of a product while at the same time making use of methods that allow for its conservation

symbiotic relationship A partnership between two species that live close together that provides benefits to both organisms

temperate forest Typical forest of the middle latitudes with temperate climates, which have four seasons: dry summers, cold winters, and rainy intermediate seasons

temperate zone The climate zone located approximately between 40 and 60 degrees latitude that is characterized as having moderate weather and climate conditions

termite An insect that lives in large colonies and eats and destroys wood

topsoil The layer of soil at the ground's surface

toucan A stocky bird with short wings, noted for its brightly colored bill. It is found in the forests of Mexico and Central and South America.

touraco Brilliantly colored African bird of the Musophagidae family

trogon The common name for the various species of tropical birds of the Trogoniformes order that have bright, shiny plumage

tropical deciduous forest A tropical forest characterized by a brief rainy season and a long dry season during which most of the trees lose their leaves

tropical monsoon forest A type of Asian deciduous tropical forest

tropical mountain forest A type of tropical forest generally characterized by the presence of conifers

tropical rain forest Typical tropical forest characterized by high rainfall and evergreen plants

tuber A type of plant with an underground stem and tiny, scalelike leaves with buds. The potato is a tuber.

undergrowth The portion of plant cover in a forest that grows low to the ground

vertebrate An animal that has a backbone

FURTHER READING

Banks, Martin. *Conserving Rain Forests*. Raintree Steck-Vaughn, 1990

Ganeri, Anita. *Explore the World of Exotic Rainforests*. Western, 1992

George, Jean C. *One Day in the Tropical Rain Forest*. HarperCollins, 1990

George, Michael. *Rain Forest*. Creative Education, 1993

Goodman, Billy. *The Rain Forest*. Little, 1992

Jones, Shirley. *Saving the Rain Forest—Why?* PPI, 1995

Landau, Elaine. *Tropical Rain Forests Around the World*. Watts, 1991

MacRae-Campbell, Linda and McKisson, Micki. *The Future of Our Tropical Rainforests*. Zephyr, 1990

Miller, Christina G. and Berry, Louise A. *Jungle Rescue: Saving the New World Tropical Rain Forests*.
  Simon & Schuster Childrens, 1991

Morris, E. and Sadler, T. *Our Rainforests and the Issues*. International Specialized Books Services, 1992

Morrison, Marion. *The Amazon Rain Forest and Its People*. Thomson Learning, 1995

Parkin, Tom. *Green Giants: Rainforests of the Pacific Northwest*. Firefly Books, 1992

The Rainforests. Trafalgar, 1992

Sayre, April P. *Tropical Rainforest*. 21st Century Books, 1994

Schmidt, A. *The Disappearing Rain Forests*. PPI, 1995

Siy, Alexandra. *The Amazon Rainforest*. Macmillan, 1992

Warburton, Lois. *Rainforests*. Lucent, 1991

Williams, Lawrence. *Jungles*. Marshall Cavendish, 1990

PICTURE CREDITS

The first number refers to the page. The number in parentheses refers to the illustration.
Photographs
U. BÄR VERLAG, Zürich (MAXIMILIEN BRUGGMANN): p. 50 ERIZZO EDITRICE, Venice (PHOTO RESEARCHERS): p. 27; (M. SARTOR): p. 49. GRANATA PRESS, Milan (J. CARVALHO): p. 46; (MARTIN HARVEY): p. 34; (OTTO ROGGE): p. 19 (3); (A. SARAGOSA): p. 18, p. 43; (PAUL STEEL): pp. 2–3 (STOCKTAKE): p. 11. EDITORIALE JACA BOOK, Milan: p. 26; (DUILIO CITI): pp. 20–21, p. 36, p. 51 (left); (RENATO MASSA) p. 19 (2), p. 33 (5); (CARLO SCOTTI): p. 8. GRAZIA NERI, Milan (HAROLDO PALO Jr.): p. 29; (José Caldas): p. 37. JEAN-JACQUES PETTER, Paris: p. 32, p. 33 (3). RITA UMBRI, Pisa: p. 33 (4). MIREILLE VAUTIER, Paris: p. 14, p. 44, p. 45, p. 47, p. 51 (right).
Color plates and drawings
EDITORIALE JACA BOOK, Milan (MAURO CAMMILLI): p. 25; (GIACINTO GAUDENZI): p. 39; (CARLO JACONO): pp. 40–41; (ALESSANDRA MICHELETTI): pp. 22–23, pp. 26–27, p. 28, pp. 30–31, pp. 34–35, p. 38, p. 40 (1, 2); (ROSALBA MORIGGIA & MARIA PIATTO): pp. 10–11, pp. 12–13, pp. 16–17; (GIULIA RE): p. 15, pp. 48–49.

Separate illustrations
pp. 4–5: A view deep inside a tropical rain forest in Tasmania, Australia
Page 8: A beautiful fossilized *Pecopteris* fern found in Bavaria, Germany, dating from the Carboniferous and Permian periods
Page 50: A coniferous forest on Baranof Island in the Alexander Archipelago, Alaska, silhouetted against the late afternoon sun
Page 51: Left: Autumn in a deciduous broadleaf forest in the Ligurian Apennines, Italy.
Right: A tropical forest halfway up the Marañon River, a tributary of the Amazon River

INDEX

Note: Page numbers in italics indicate illustrations.

Adaptations
    Amerindian groups, *38*
    animals, 24
    baboons, 32
    to environment, 39
    gorilla, 32
    parrots, 34
    South American monkeys, 31
    three-toed sloth, *27*
Aerial roots, 16
    of *Ficus*, 21
Africa
    Indian monsoon forest in, *17*
    monkeys of, 31
    monsoon forests in, 18
    mountain forests in, 18
    tropical forest environments in, *26*
    tropical rain forests in, 10, *12–13*
African hoopoes, 24
Afro-Asian hornbills, 24, *25*
Agriculture
    in Grande Caracas, *44*
    as threat to forests, *12, 13*
    using land for, *15*
    See also Farms; Livestock farming;
        Nomadic agriculture
Aloe striata flower, *20*
Altitude
    and forest, 16
    and vegetation of mountain forests, 18
Amazon basin, 9, 16, 50
    Amerindian groups in, *38, 40*
    range of species in, 20
Amazon parrots, 34
Amazon village, everyday life in, *39*
Amphibians, in tropical forest, 24
Anacondas (snakes), 24
Andes cordillera, mountain forests in, 18
Angiosperms, in tropical rain forests, 20–21
Angola, tropical forest in, *13*
Animals
    adaptations of, 24
    and nutrient reserves, 14
    as pollinators, 24
    restrictive reproduction of, 24
Anteaters, tree-dwelling, 24
Antelope, savanna vs. forest, 38
Anthropoids, *31*
    in tropical forest, 32
Anthropomorphs, ground-dwelling, *31*
Anthurium andraeanum, 20

Ants
    army, 24
    leafcutter, 24
Asia
    lowland tropical rain forest in, *25*
    monkeys of, 31
    monsoon forests in, *18, 19*
    tropical forests in, *13*
Australia, tropical forests in, *13*

Baboon mask, *26*
Baboons, *31*
    adaptations of, 32
    of Africa *(Papio cynocephalus), 33*
    habitat of, 30
Baka pygmies, *40*
Bald ouakari *(Cacajao calvo), 33*
Bamboo, *21,* 24
Bananas *(Musa sapientum), 15*
    See also Wild bananas
Bangladesh, tropical forest in, *13*
Barbary ape, 30
Bark, tree, 39
Beaks, toucan, *27*
Bearded pig *(Sus barbatus),* 48
Beef production, South vs. North America, *47*
Belize, tropical rain forest in, *12*
Benin, tropical forest in, *12*
Bills
    as climbing aid, 34, *35*
    uses of, in parrots, 34
Biodiversity, reduction of, 48
Biomass, 9
Birds
    endangered, 42
    and seed dispersal, 24
    as tree-dwellers, 24
Birthrate, human, 42
Black-headed lemurs, 32
Boas (snakes), 24
Bolivia, tropical forests in, *12*
Borneo, 16, 48, 50
    hunters of, *38*
    mountain forest in, *16, 18*
Brachiating, 30, 31
Brachiation, *30*
    and origin of humans, 31–32
Bramble thickets, 20
Brazil, tropical rain forest in, *12*
Brunei, Borneo
    number of tree species in, 20
    tropical forest in, *13*
Budgerigars, 34

Buffalo, savanna vs. forest, 38
Burma, tropical forest in, *13*
Buttresses, 21

Calathea setosa, 20
Cambodia, 50
    tropical forest in, *13*
Cameroon, tropical forests in, *13, 40*
Canopy, 16
    density of, in tropical forest, 20
    Klong-Nakah forest station, 24
    in lowland rain forest, 18
    of mountain forests, 18
    thinning of, 48
Captivity, effect of, on parrots, 36
Carbon dioxide, 9
Carboniferous period, forest of, *10*
Caribbean, tropical rain forests in, *12*
Catarrhine group, *31, 33*
    See also Old World monkeys
Central America
    Indian monsoon forest in, *17*
    monkeys in, 31
    monsoon forests in, 18
    tropical rain forests in, 10, *12, 13*
Cercopithecidae, 31
Chain reaction, 48
Chimpanzee *(Pan troglodytes), 31,* 32
    savanna vs. forest, *38*
China, tropical forest in, *13*
Ciperaceae family, 21
Cities, founding of, in tropical forests, *43*
Clearings
    monsoon forests, 18, *19*
    in tropical forests, *39, 40*
Climate, and forests, 16
Climax environments, 50
Clouds, and mountain forests, 18
Cocoons, 24
Coevolution, 48
Collared parakeets, 34
Colombia, tropical rain forest in, *12*
Colonists, *46*
Color vision, 30
Congo, *26*
    tropical forest in, *13*
Conservation, efforts toward, 42
Conservation biologists, 9
Conservation International agency,
    conservation diagram of, *49*
Corn *(Zea mays), 15*
Costa Rica
    seed dispersal in, *49*
    tropical rain forest in, *12*